# I'M PERFECT. NEITHER IS LIFE

# I'm Perfect.
# Neither is Life

By ya boy
Shea D.

Shea Deignan

# 1

I'm Perfect. Neither is Life.

To my family and friends that all played a part in my life for the better and for the worst. To make those experiences and challenges unlike any other. My amazing wife Kristina and our son Shea Jr, continue to inspire me to be better than the next day!

September 30th, 2004.

The thirtieth of September in 2004

30 Sep 2004.

No matter how I look at it, it was one of the worst days of my life.

What's yours?

Do you even remember where you were born? Do you remember asking your parents anything about if they were your real parents at some point?

Born in Providence, RI in 1991 Women and Infants Hospital over by Eddy Street is where almost everyone is born in Rhode Island. What I do remember is moving from city to city in Rhode Island, getting in trouble, being a "good" kid, and excelling in a lot of other activities. I will start with my earliest childhood memories and that is running into the table at the age of 5 chasing after my brother and getting knocked out around the corner real quick. When I was a child I used to hate telling that story because I would be embarrassed that I had gotten a scar right above my right eyebrow, by running into a table. Classy. Now I don't have a problem with it, I just feel that it's cool to have scars now than I did when I was younger.

At a very young age I felt out of place, as if I didn't belong.

I felt that in my life at times that I was unable to be a child, life was moving too fast and I felt that I had to grow up a lot faster than I should.

Working hard to accomplish a Bachelor's degree and a Master's degree, something I could never imagine in my lifetime.
What were my motivations?
What are yours?

I grew up with three brothers John, James, and Ryan. Had a mother Susan and father Michael. At one point we were all living together when I was really young. Ryan is six years older than me, James is 8 years older than me, and John is 11 years older than me. Living together wasn't much of a memory, not really knowing what happened and I would have to live through photos that were taken, and my family telling their stories. There were two houses that I remember our family living together, one on Ruggles closer to the north end of Providence and one house in the west end on Linwood ave in Providence, RI.

Down the road on Linwood Ave at Bucklin park my brothers and I all played for the local football team called the West End Intruders. The field was made of low cut grass and dirt patches. I remember going to practice one day, not feeling well at all, throwing up all over the place I still wanted to go because I loved the sport that much, even my coach would tell me to stop running laps. I would just nod my head and say, "I'm ok coach" and kept running. Then at one point I was over the weight limit once I got to peewee level where helmets and pads were required, I did not have a chance to play tackle football until High School. I couldn't play and only practice, I enjoyed playing football because of the commitment the team makes, remembering my focus during the games rather than who was at the games at times. I felt I was in my own world for those couple of hours playing at a young age and nothing else had mattered from start to finish.

Growing up in Providence was amazing, I love Providence to this day, familiarizing myself with all the local food spots, corner stores and even down the street on Progress Ave a family sold icey's. Coconut was my favorite flavor. I lived everywhere with my mother, Providence, Woonsocket, Middletown, Newport. I often have to recall where I went to school at moments because of the amount of times that I have moved. For instance, 1st grade was Charles N Fortes in Providence, 2nd grade started at Charles N Fortes, then finished at Underwood in Newport, 3rd grade Webster Ave in Providence, 4th Grade Globe Park elementary in Woonsocket and Forest Ave in Middletown, 5th and 6th grade at Joseph H Gaudet Middle School in Middletown, started 7th Grade at Aldrich Junior High in Warwick, Finished 7th grade in Woonsocket, 8th Grade back in Providence at Esek Hopkins Middle School and finished my High school education for all 4 years at Textron Chambers of Commerce Academy. Every time I look back on it, it is mind boggling how to even think I learned, socialize and even exist to this day to survive uncertainty for many years. Living in different areas unfortunately showed me that things were not necessarily the same in all parts of the state. In addition, kids all behaved differently depending on where you lived. For instance, there was so much energy coming from kids and not having to pay much attention in class in Woonsocket, whereas Middletown was all business and kids were all attentive in class engaged in learning with less distractions.

Why would you think that is?

At a very young age I put my mother through a heart attack, at one point when we were in downtown Providence, RI, we were walking around and looked like my mother was on a mission to get something accomplished. I had upset my mother and she had started walking faster, unsure of what I had said to make her walk faster but I could not keep up with her so I stopped walking with her. I started walking into stores because I was bored and I waited in Kennedy Plaza which is the bus station that traveled throughout the state, waiting at the bus stop without my mother. A police officer comes walking over and says "is there a She-uh Deignan?" I look over and say "that's me". We start walking over to the police station where the mayor's office is and my mother is crying, and in my head I am like why is she upset when she was upset with me and started walking fast where I couldn't keep up. Another officer takes out the handcuffs and starts yelling at me to play that bad cop role, making me cry as my mother is calming down.

Living with just my mother at this time on Linwood Ave, in a different house where my brothers lived elsewhere. A couple blocks over, I started 1st grade at Charles N Fortes in Providence, Rhode Island on the west end, it was one of the first places that I knew I loved applesauce. The teacher had made it for the students in class and the smell of cinnamon and granny smith apples were just amazing. I couldn't say that I left first grade with an impression to this day other than applesauce. I remember crying and the assistant teacher had to calm me down, and I again had done something to piss my mother off and she ripped my homework up while she was waiting in the car. I was crying like it was a bad dream, feeling embarrassed in front of my teacher. I still felt out of place as if I didn't belong, I have no idea why, I couldn't explain it. I felt I was going to school just to go to school. I have always had this feeling.

2$^{nd}$ grade at Charles N Fortes elementary school for the first couple of weeks which had seemed very blurry at that point. There were some kids I met there that led to some school friendships with Steve and Martin in 2nd grade at Charles N' Fortes, during recess where we would play two handed touch football and nothing else as if we were all planning on making it to the NFL. One street over was the recreation center and where the West End Intruders community football team for kids play. What felt like after a couple of days of starting 2nd grade I moved to Newport, where I have not been before unsure what it was going to be like there since I have been in Providence clost to my family all this time.

This was the first time I moved from Providence and further away from my brothers and father. At that age I never asked why, I just did what I was told. Moving to Newport was so weird the first time because we were living in a 3rd floor apartment near the bus terminal, with no furniture but a bed I would share with my mother. I used to wake up extra early. It would still be dark outside and I would take the RIPTA bus with my mother so that I would get dropped off at Underwood Elementary School. Unsure of where or what my mother was going to do considering she was the only one on the bus with the bus driver when I got dropped off at the school. I arrived earlier than all the other students so I just waited outside until it was time to go into class. It was the same room for all of the different subjects and only went outside for physical education, which was hot potato and basketball from time to time

At one point in Newport, where my mother and I were staying, there was one older woman with dark red hair and I do not remember exactly if we were living with, or if it was the person we were renting from who had stopped by the place frequently. But one day my mother was mad and I couldn't tell why until she screamed "that woman stole my money!". We never went back to that place and moved to St. Lucy's Hearth in Middletown. St. Lucy's Hearth is a women's shelter, which would allow women to stay there who are in need of a place to stay along with their children. As a child I thought it was fantastic, there were people of all ages, interacting with kids older and younger than me. Each family had their own room, and there was a playground out in the back with a basketball hoop, sand box, concrete to play hopscotch, double dutch, all fenced in so no one could sneak in or sneak out. Met some really cool people there and at times I felt alone, unsure of what I was missing. Trying to figure out the life of being a child and not really seeing my brothers, but also never had a sense to myself to wonder where they were or why they weren't here or we weren't there with them. I felt that it would be a conversation my mother would not have wanted to talk about. I never asked about it. The school year I was learning to write in cursive, given a caterpillar and watch it grow into a beetle, not remembering many of the kids' names during my time at Underwood. It was another school with another group of kids that I did not plan on making friends with. Unsure of what was to come as the year went on. Finishing second grade at Underwood Elementary School felt like another pit stop in my life that I had to get through just to make it another year.

Summer is here and I am going to my father's for the summer.

Was this the plan all along?

Summer was great, no school, we would celebrate Ryan and James birthdays, full of water balloon fights, and water guns, especially the super soakers (I was always jealous of never getting one for my birthday). I would wake up early and walk to Flats basketball court, where I would be the only one on the court because of how early I would get up. Flats is the basketball court that you can see right off route 10 in the distance. I would say that is where I built upon my basketball game and where I learned the most from. I would sometimes spend most of my days there just shooting around waiting for other kids to play games like around the world, a game of Horse, one on one's or watch the older kids play full court games. Summers would also consist of walking to the corner store to get my father the Providence Journal on Saturdays or Sundays, mainly to check movie times if there was a good movie coming out. We would drive around looking for yard sales, go to Rocky Hill Flea Market where people would sell those bootleg movies on DVD's with people walking in front of the camera. Or you would be able to get a bong or pipe if need be. Felt that there was just a lot lifted off of my shoulders when it came to the summer. My grandmother (Gram) and grandfather (Don) from my father's side, would pick Ryan and I up some days and take us to the beach, before going they would give us a call and ask what sandwiches we would want and bologna and cheese was always my preferred choice with mustard. Yum!

Down the street on Progress Ave, one friend of mine at the time, Joey, we would consistently hang out since we were close in age. We would spend days together hanging out and playing basketball playing football in the street. Occasionally I would go to his place and we would play Playstation, or we would play basketball at Flats. We would usually hang out all summer since there wasn't anything else going on around the neighborhood.

Never asked but what were my brothers up to? They were older so I just figured they were either hanging out with their friends or what not.

It was getting closer to school starting and I didn't even think to ask about what was happening with school and who I was going to be living with. School comes back around for third grade I went to Charles N Fortes for two days then on the third day, my dad excitedly says to Joey's mother on our way into school like he was celebrating a championship, that I am going to Webster Ave school, which was down the street from where we lived so it is easy to walk to and from. Again I didn't ask any questions why I was going there and not living with my mother. Webster Ave, another school with more kids not remembering their names other than Joey. One of the first times that I heard someone having eczema, kids being kids in third grade saying that there were eggs in their head. That poor girl cried thinking that a bunch of third grade kids convinced her that she had eggs in her head. At that very moment I thought that was the dumbest joke, yet everyone laughed at it.

What the hell was the teacher doing? Who knows, probably just babysitting the class. This was the time that kids would say eww cooties, and whoever smelt it dealt it. I mean what a time to be alive. Red light green light was a popular recess game at the time, along with simon says. In today's world everyone is talking in code, rotflmao, idek, js, wtf, no cap, and whatever else you can think of.

Surprise, I did not finish up the school year at Webster Ave and went back to living with my mother for the rest of third grade and some of 4th grade attending Globe Park elementary school in Woonsocket. Living in Woonsocket for the first time was interesting to say the least, another area in Rhode Island that I am trying to get accustomed to. Third grade was a short period of time at this point, and again what did I take away from my time in the third grade? Nothing.

It is now summer and living on the third floor is hot as hell in a house next to the restaurant named Al's. Walking in with my mother as she orders food to eat and after we were given this monster of a to go box, I remember sitting on the steps outside with my mother having a plain mustard burger from Al's, was one of the most peaceful moments in life that I ever had. Nothing was said, we just ate the burger. Going to school in Woonsocket was definitely a different experience, always felt gloomy and buildings looked old like the town was in a war. I was getting involved in sports again and for basketball this time which was played at Woonsocket Middle School with some old creaky floors. It was a short league or I just wasn't able to attend the rest of the games. The summer in Woonsocket felt hot and I didn't seem to feel refreshed that summer like I couldn't get to the beach or go swimming in a pool or anything to cool off.

Fourth Grade had begun still in Woonsocket.

My mother and I were at one of her friends' place

and I started vomiting and had stomach pains. I could not keep any food down, would eat Ramen, and that came right out. I was over the toilet the entire time, and I was telling my mother that I needed to go to the hospital. My mother would not believe me and I just kept vomiting and vomiting, which was just liquid. My stomach felt like what a towel must feel when you would ring it out to get rid of the water. I was saying to myself what in the hell is wrong with me. Eventually my mother must have been sick of me complaining and brought me to Hasbro Children's Hospital and it was my Appendix. I had to have an appendectomy, removal of the appendix, and I was scared as shit. I was like what, why do I have to have surgery at 9 years old? I remember the white dot that was on the x-ray that the doctor pointed out. I could just look back and remember the time my brother John said that his appendix had burst which is not necessarily what you want when you have appendicitis because it can cause complications when trying to remove the appendix. After waiting to go into the operating room, I must have passed out or they had already given me something because the next thing I know, I wake up in the bright pink operating room with a oxygen mask over my mouth. Eyes open and reaching out to some-one in a white coat in the operating room saying "I can't breathe", with the mask on. Next thing, I saw a needle being injected into my IV line and then I was out cold.

AHHHHHH!

I am Screaming in pain after the surgery being sent to my room for the rest of the night. Late at night a nurse comes into the room telling me that if I am in pain to push this button to help ease the pain. Well little did I know that if I keep pressing the button it is not going to work properly. Looking back, why in the world would you give a 9 year old pain medication, let alone a button to push. Either way the nurse was sick and tired of me pressing the nurse call button to keep coming into the room letting her know I was in pain. My mother was sleeping in the chair next to me in the room with a jacket to keep her warm overnight. The next day I was told to pee in a bottle because I was not getting out of that bed after surgery. Of course my brothers and my dad came to visit me including Junia who was dating my father at the time, and I had to pee. They are all standing there as Junia turns around as I pee in a damn bottle because I couldn't get out of bed yet. AWKWARD!!!

I always felt that there was an obligation when people were in the hospital that people who cared had to go see you. Is that just out of caring or just being polite? Do people expect you to do things like that?

Well I had to be able to get up and move around the room before being discharged from the hospital. Trying to stand was such a struggle, walking was painful, standing for a period of time was another pain. A bonus to staying at Hasbro Children's Hospital was that they had the Nintendo 64 and played some video games for some time as long as it was available.

The day has arrived where I am being discharged from the hospital, in pain. My Mother's friend comes to pick us up and let me tell you, getting into the backseat of an old ass Ford Bronco where there is no back door and having to climb into the back seat through the front after just getting discharged and being able to just walk around. That was just dandy. Finally go home to rest and get back to school. I showed up to school the next day and every day the first thing we did in the morning of class was complete a word search puzzle. I bring my completed word search puzzle to my teacher's desk, and my teacher asks why I have been absent from school. "I had my appendix removed." My teacher says, "you should have told us we would have come to visit, are you ok?" At that moment I was shocked. I answered, "yeah I am ok, thank you." I went back to my desk and still think about it till this day why my teacher would even go that route to visit a student who was in the hospital. I only interacted with my teacher in school, I only spoke when spoken to in class, answered questions I thought I knew when they were asked. Would she visit any student if they were in the hospital or was I the exception?

Later that school year in fourth grade I moved back to St. Lucy's Hearth with my mother to finish off 4th grade at Forest Ave in Middletown. Again who am I entering this school and who are these kids who have known each other for years already. Recess is still a thing in 4th grade and people were gathering around the diamond field getting ready to play kickball. Well it's another sport that I can get down with, captains are being chosen and I am getting picked last on a team. First off, I can kick a damn ball there is no science to it, I throw the ball pretty good too. Well I am the new kid, no one knows who the hell I am, and I feel insulted but not enough to really care that first day but I do afterwards. Hanging out with other kids outside of school didn't necessarily happen because people weren't allowed to come over to St. Lucy's Hearth unless you lived there. I wasn't that close with any of the kids to even hang out with anyone outside of school so it was whoever was at "home". Well, going to Forest Ave was only temporary anyways because 5th grade was middle school in Middletown.

5th grade at Joseph H Gaudet Middle School was another journey with the suspense being built up by other kids moving up to middle school. Like sweet we are getting older and getting closer to the cooler stuff that we see older kids do when they reach that age. Getting out of school earlier, meeting more people, or whatever you can imagine middle schoolers wanting to do. That was not the middle school life that I had.

My mother at this point was working at St. Lucy's Hearth, and living there at my age was a little different, especially since my mother was now an employee there. People had to be careful what was said around me and I had to be careful what I did and said around others. I was the only child there whose mother worked there.

St. Lucy's Hearth layout was simple and one stairway to this day I hated for the mere fact that people who smoked sat in this stairway and it was like walking through the smoking section at a casino just clouds of smoke just to get into the backyard. My mother and the morning workers would sit there frequently and just smoke those Newports and Mystic 100s. I purposely would walk outside consistently and cough hoping they would get the hint. Well they never quit smoking. The other benefit of my mother working there was that she was able to smoke in her room. Not a perk for me. Most mornings would consist of me waking up waiting for the bus for school with another kid who lived in these apartment complexes nearby. Would have to wait on West Main Road across the street from where the old Ames used to be which is now other stores and Staples. We would sometimes play Pokemon or Yu Gi Oh while waiting for the school bus. It was the last stop before arriving at school and almost like that moment in Forest Gump when he gets on the bus and you are just looking for a seat to sit down on. Well that awkward moment where you have to sit next to someone you never met on a bus where you are just trying to make it to school without actually having a conversation but enough to make the rest of the ride not awkward. Some mornings at school I would have enough time to play a game of suicide. Throwing a ball, whether it would be a racquetball, or tennis ball off the wall and everyone had to run before the person caught it and chucked it at the people running towards the wall. Being a victim of a racquetball at your back is not something you want early in the morning.

There were 6 teachers that I had in total, one would teach English and History, one teacher for each of the following, Science, Math, Art, Phys Ed., and one for Japanese. Not sure who thought that teaching a fifth grader Japanese was a great idea because I do not remember anything other than how to spell my name which is probably a lie. The teacher must have sold them on the fact that she could get us to speak Japanese fluently by the time we were done in middle school. Doubt it. There were days I woke up and said I didn't feel like going to school. I would tell my mother I didn't feel well and pretend with that fake sick voice like Ferris Bueller's Day Off. She would either believe me or didn't care, I wouldn't go to school and I would get to eat chicken noodle soup for the day. Yum. I would also pretend to be sick so I could watch The Price Is Right at home and avoid having to go to school. I didn't find school challenging at this point and I felt bored. It seemed to be more of a social event for me to get a chance to meet and talk with kids my age. Although I did very well in school, it wasn't something I woke up excited to go to but felt that I had to because everyone else did.

One time during homeroom, I was sitting in the back of the class and I didn't care. I had to fart and man it was bad. I was sent to the nurses office. Never farted in school again.

During Phys Ed., we had to run a mile, and we were timed, I said to myself why in the world are you torturing us we just want to play. Running that mile was the worst, it was on the track in the back of the school and kids were doing that with ease and here I am just trying to catch my breath and make it around the track. Well at that point there was one kid who was bigger than me, twice my size and he told the teacher that the maker on his hand had come off so he ran his four laps. Not by chance that man was beating me in time and the teacher believed him. So I made sure to make it a point every time we ran that mile that he and I were running near each other so that he couldn't cheat again. Petty. School is promoting career day, and here I am like what the hell am I going to dress up as for career day like what I want to be when I get older. I didn't have a suit and tie or anything nice to wear so I wore my baseball outfit that I would wear to my little league games. No one said that there were supposed to be people speaking to us on career day like damn. Kids at school asked me why I wore my uniform. I said I had a game today. That was a lie.

Summer time.

Well I went to spend the week at my dads in Providence, RI on Progress Ave during the summer, which just consisted of hanging out with my friend Joey down the street, playing basketball at the Flats court. My father was bringing me back to St. Lucy's Hearth, well my father stopped the car in the open parking lot behind the church so he and I could walk and talk. Normally he would drop me off in the front of the building.

Was I in trouble?

Did he not want me to visit him in the summer anymore because of Junia?

I had no clue what this was all about and it must have been important for him to say this to me because Junia was in the car sitting there waiting for my father to come back to the car.

My dad then proceeds to say to me, "you know how two people have children? Well, I am not your father. I just wanted to let you know and I still love you." That felt like the longest walk I had ever taken in my life and my heart just broke.

What do you mean you're not my father?
What the hell was I calling you dad for then?
Who am I?

I was waiting outside of St. Lucy's Hearth for my mother to open the door to see me balling my eyes out. My mother asked, "what's wrong?"

"He's not my father!" in a whiny 10 year olds voice.

My mother was livid, like some dark secret she did not want me to know about. She called my father back and was screaming on the phone. Turns her chair towards me and asks, "well what do you want to know?"

What do I ask? Like shit, I just had a grown man who I call my father (still do to this day), tell me that he isn't my father and you want me to ask questions.

"What's his name?"

"Mikal"

Are you kidding me? My father's name is Michael, and my biological father's name is Mikal.

Well that was about it and the conversation my mother and I had about my biological father.

Call me naive, blind or whatever, but I never looked at my skin and said wow I am different from my brothers. They are and will always be my brothers. When I was younger and kids would see me and pictures of my brothers, they would ask why am I darker than them.

"I tan easier than them" I lived and died by that answer until I actually realized.

6th grade was a great year I felt like, going to the same school, same friends, and the only thing different were my teachers. I remember one of my assignments for history class, learning Greek mythology and I had to make a rap on Poseidon.

My name is Posiedon the god of sea,

Zeus and Pluto are my only homies.

That is all I remember from the rap but there was a little more. I know I should have become a rapper, I would have made it!

I was going to join this academic team in 6th grade where only a few of us were chosen to compete similar to an academic competition. There were three students and a teacher, we would practice on a computer answering questions until competition against other schools started. I was unable to actually compete because my mother, my brother John and I had flown down to attend James's graduation from boot camp in Fort Knox, Kentucky. I will say I was not a fan of flying on a plane for the first time. I was hyperventilating and had to sit in the middle between them on the plane. I was upset about missing the competition because I just wanted to always compete. Not as much as being disappointed in not joining the band because my mother said she couldn't afford to pay the rental fee for the instrument. I thought about playing the saxophone because my brother John had played it in high school.

Fort Knox was interesting, the hail that would come down and break someone's car window and people would think someone had broken into their car. The food choices were not something I was interested in.

Grits, eww. It was very muggy, and felt musty in Kentucky, as if the air was thick. I was just told to scream when we heard James's name get called. We waited outside the building to get a chance to talk to James before it was a while that I would see him again. At Christmas time my mother told me that my brother James was being deployed and was extremely upset because I associated the bad when it comes to being deployed.

I had this teacher in the 6th grade, where it would just be a few of us sitting around a table in a Library, and it was awkward and creepy because he would talk real softly and didn't really teach anything. He looked like someone who would have been a serial killer and may have gotten away with it.

There was a day in 6th grade that allowed the students to visit the 7th grade teachers, and get a better understanding of what the classes would be like and what you would be learning. The 7th grade teacher said we would dissect a frog and I thought that would have been fun.

In my math class I would pretend that I didn't understand the material that we were learning just to get out of the classroom because I was bored. There would be a teacher's assistant to bring some of the students to another room just to go over other examples. I had no business being there. School wasn't necessarily hard, I was bored, and wanted to socialize. I won't sit here and say that I was a genius and knew everything, I felt that I was not being challenged enough to care and I would do enough just to get by. There was one teacher, Mrs. Searcy, where I had the Greek mythology class, and social studies. She would challenge everyone and I enjoyed her class much more.

At one point I had a job delivering newspapers to this apartment complex on Saturdays and Sundays, to this apartment complex that was practically right next to St. Lucy's Hearth. I had to make sure those newspapers were delivered by 8am on Saturdays and by 6am on Sundays. It was cool until I lost my keys one time and had to leave the newspapers outside each building rather than the apartment number door. Once in a while my mother would drive me on Sundays because I had to get up early in the morning to fold the newspapers, and deliver them. I would race alongside the car and she would tell me how fast I was going. 15 miles per hour homie.

Well here comes another summer and I am going to a summer camp somewhere overnight for some time. My mother drops me off down the street from St. Lucy's Hearth to wait for the bus to bring us to the camp grounds. It was only for a week but it was not anything special. My mother probably just wanted me to get away for some time in the summer. Well when it was time to leave the camp, get dropped off at the same place we got picked up, I was not given any instructions from my mother on what to do. Well

I waited for maybe an hour and I just walked to St. Lucy's Hearth. It was maybe a half a mile away, and I was carrying my bag of clothes and I got to the facility and rang the buzzer. No one had a key because they didn't want anyone to be able to have access to a women's shelter.

Well one of the staff members had opened up the door and was surprised to see me.

My mother wasn't there.

Don't remember if it was the next day or the following but I felt so out of place. I could tell the other families were asking me where my mother was and I did not know. I asked myself why isn't she here? Did she forget?

Did she not care? At least that is how I felt then.

Needless to say her bosses were not happy with her not being there when I came back and on the move we went again.

I actually thought that I would continue school in Middletown but on my way to live with my father who had recently bought a place in Warwick.

Where did my mother go?

Another year, another school at Aldrich Jr High which was right across the Walmart on Post Road. This was a turning point for me during my time here. I had met people that I am friends with to this day and not what I was expecting considering that I moved so many times and making friends was just not my thing because I was not sure where I was going to be next year. Well this was the first time that I had smoked weed. I thought I was cool hiding in the woods with my friends to smoke a bowl and to be honest looking back at it. It was some trash weed.

That is why I started stealing money from my dad and my step mother Junia. I mean it was an act that is embarrassing to think about to this day. There were times that I wanted to fit in with my friends, go to the movies, the mall, and even smoke more weed. I felt the need to fit in somewhere at that point in my life, because if I didn't now, what the hell was I going to end up doing with my life.

It was a waste of my time.

A turning point in my life when my father found out I was stealing money from him and Junia. He called DCYF.

I remember speaking to the woman from DCYF about what I was doing with the money. I lied, said I was buying video games. Of course they knew it was a lie because I did not have a game system. When I was coming back home from just playing basketball with my friends, my dad yelling at me "DOES IT SAY STUPID ACROSS MY FUCKING FOREHEAD?!" That was the last straw.

Conversations with the woman from DCYF had

continued, now I am going back to live with my mother back in Woonsocket, RI to finish 7th grade. Before I went to live back with my mother, I was supposed to be suspended for not attending detention after punching a kid in the arm. The principal at the time was Mr. Habershaw, who I thought was a decent person at school, never gave him much trouble other than not attending detention. Before leaving Mr. Habershaw wanted to speak with my mother and wanted said how I was a good kid. Again what did that mean?

Back in Woonsocket was night and day compared to living in Warwick. In Woonsocket kids did not want to be in school, it was also closer to summer and they were excited to finish school for the year. Being at that school felt like there was chaos in my brain but not too much that I was able to go to school and go home.

My mother and I were having arguments, I definitely felt frustrated but unsure of why. Maybe because we also did not have air conditioning and it was just muggy inside the apartment complex.

I would spitefully tell my mother that my brothers are not even my brothers (using my thought of us not having the same biological father). I would sit there and sulk just feeling angry inside.

I was just so angry and frustrated at everything.

Well to say the least my mother ends up going to the hospital for an unknown reason this time. I have to go to a group home right across the street from where I used to live when I was going to elementary school. We would get dropped off by a van

Living at that group home was almost relaxing, but very eye opening. It was only for males, and there were structures for living there. Keep your room clean, complete your chores, help cook meals, participate in any activities that they plan. It was definitely to keep us busy. Then by the end of the week you would be graded and depending on your grade you would get a certain amount of cash.

The people that I met were either without families, needed to be adopted to get out of the group home, or families couldn't keep them at home. It felt like a dysfunctional family because we all knew we had to get along just to get by. Of course there were moments that we all hated each other, or were jealous because of one thing or another but it is what it is.

I was there for a short time frame because my mother was only in the hospital for maybe a couple weeks. Then I was out of the group home for the next week or so. Then I went back because my mother went back to the hospital. During the summer at the group home it was boring, walking around the block of the house, playing basketball in the back, and that was only part of my summer. Not knowing what was going on at the hospital with my mother, I was going to summer camp for the day while at the group home because they did not want a bunch of teenage boys sitting in the house going nuts. No matter where I went I always looked to see where I fit. Not to fit in. I did not change myself for other people to like me. Why did I belong here with everyone else that is in this group home? I needed to ask the house manager for a voucher for clothes, and had to ask when I would be able to go see my mother because there was a point I didn't hear from anyone from my family. One woman, Joan, who used to work with my mother at St. Lucy's Hearth would visit my mother at Miriam Hospital and one time my brother John was there as well. It was awkward because Joan wanted me to go outside with her while she smoked a cigarette. I thought they knew I hated cigarettes and smoke, but I stood there inhaling cancer not knowing why my mother was in the hospital. Yet I am outside with Joan, wonderful.

At the end of visiting I ended up back at the group home, it's still summer and I got along with just about everyone at the group home or at least I tried to. I just felt so weird because I thought I had a family and why am I not living with anyone? It was my fault wasn't it?

One day I went back to visiting my mother at Miriam Hospital, and my brother John was there as well as Joan. Joan decides to go out for a smoke and I am in the room with my mother and my brother John.

My mother tells me she has cancer.

My.

Mother.

Has.

Cancer.

Why? What? How? When?

I cried, as did my mother and John.

After my mother told me, she then asks if I want to live with John.

If I said no, would I stay at the group home? Why would I even say no? Do I have a choice? Do I dare ask?

This felt like the longest summer that I ever had. There was a lot going on and I started to feel more uncertainty for really the first time in my life because my mother has cancer. What does that mean?

I knew my brother lived in providence, but where do I go to school? I go to school for one year in 8th grade then off to High school. Who am I?

My mother is now moved to a nursing home facility in Woonsocket because they had given her six months to live. At this point I am living with John on Coggeshall St in Providence, RI in an apartment. We would go visit from time to time, to go check in on her and it looked like she had accepted it and was enjoying time with her friends and family. She had pictures of her sons like headshots for an acting portfolio lined up on the wall.

I had just started school at Esek Hopkins Middle School for 8th grade and new people, new teachers and a new chapter. It felt like I was learning what school was like all over again because every environment is different. Who will my friends be? What classes do I have? Will any of them be interesting? My brother James who was in the Military had shown up one day randomly at our place knowing our mother was sick.

School had started late August right before Labor Day.

What I remember that day which felt like a movie was that we were looking for our brother Ryan who was working at Stop and Shop at the time and needed him to get out of work to see our mother for one last time. Three brothers on a mission to make sure we were there one last time.

There are certain smells that you never forget, and one that makes me cringe every time I even get a whiff of that smell. The smell of inpatient areas especially long term and short term facilities. It smells like death to me.

A care team had come to visit my mother, a therapist and an oncologist letting us know that her breathing will start to slow down and then that will be it. We all stood around just watching her take in her last breath and the last time that I saw my mother struggle and in pain. We grabbed the nurses to confirm that she was no longer breathing, nodding their head in acknowledgement she is dead.

Whatever time it was at night, we were spending the last few minutes as my brother James closed her eyelids as a final goodbye, and he walked straight over to me to give me a hug. I stood there frozen. We waited until the undertakers arrived to take her body and we left the facility.

All I could do was cry, I hid my face in an Eddie Jones Miami Heat Jersey to just cry because I did not know what to do. Sitting on the bed next to my mother, my brothers all in the room it just felt like that we all had an uncertainty of what was going to happen next without our mother. Maybe it was just me.

What was life going to be like without our mother?

Is it going to get easier?

Will she be happier because she is no longer in pain?

How much will I miss her?

Will I miss her?

What will I remember about my mother?

September 30th, 2004.

The thirtieth of September in 2004

30 Sep 2004

We ended up having a service for my mother at Agape in Woonsocket. There were people there that I knew and people I did not. My mother's family whom I have never met was there. One of her sisters came over to speak to us and showed us her parents at one of the tables like they wanted distance from us. Ok do you not want to know who I am, or care who I am. Why did you even show up? I could not keep it together, my father came over to me and he started crying. It was a space I have never seen him in before.

I had to return back to school and I do not re-member much of school work, home work, but most of the mornings before school to play tag football. I never wanted to go on any of the field trips that my classmates were going on, I stayed behind and went to class being the only one and essentially hung out with the teachers. The year flew by. I couldn't tell you any exciting projects I completed, I had failed a quarter in computer class which was just watching youtube videos and playing video games. John was in the Philippines, and his girlfriend Julie was watching me and I gave her attitude when she asked about my failing grade. She had to call John to try and get me to calm down and not act like a jerk, with the time difference he must have been woken up. At the time it was difficult for me to trust women, because I only really knew one, and it was a tough time listening to women to tell me what to do and listening to them. So I would say I was not very kind to Julie at times.

That year flew by in 8th grade, and the graduat-ing ceremony seemed cheesy to me and everyone's family came to celebrate. It was John and Julie at the time that came and I was thinking that I felt that I could not be appreciative enough to appreciate that moment. Someone is there for me. During the summer of 8th grade I would go back to Warwick and hang out with some friends that I had met when I was going to Aldrich. The summers would consist of drinking alcohol and smoking weed. I had also started drinking alcohol with my friends, playing beer pong in my friends basement. His family didn't seem to care about us bringing a bunch of alcohol downstairs and blasting music so that is where my first taste of beer, vodka, whiskey and all. At some points we were playing beer pong with rum rather than beer. So I have been drunk and buzzed at the age of 13.

Before the year had ended, I knew what high school I was going to and at the time it was called Textron Chambers of Commerce Academy. My brothers James and Ryan had gone there, my brother John went to Classical High School. Apparently I was not smart enough (based on the test that they had given students who wanted to go to Classical High School). Whatever, it was either I go to Hope High School, or I go to Textron. So I decided to go to Textron which had summer school for freshmen.

So it was a short summer for me, I did not know what was in store for me honestly, again a new school with a new set of classmates that I was going to meet all over again and who knew what was going to happen there. This was the first school that I was able to start and finish there from the 9th grade to 12th grade.

I felt I was getting adjusted in high school, meeting other kids although I didn't really hang out with any of them after school, I went back to Warwick over the weekend and would hang out with them. I have felt angry and aggravated some days in school. One day I told my math teacher Mr. Lelygian that he is "bitch ass motherfucker" in the middle of class. He gave me an attitude and felt that I didn't deserve it. John had heard about it and told me to write an apology letter and to say that I was sorry.

After 9th grade was finished, I felt bored and wanted to do something else and I wanted to play football, I have always had that dream of playing football. Yes of course maybe the NFL one day but It was not something I set my mind out to because I didn't know where I was going to be the next day or the next year because I felt that I was always going to be on the move. My brother John did a great job of being able to support me and stay in Providence so that we did not move anywhere which I felt that I have done all my life moving from place to place. So the summer of 9th grade I went to the Providence School department to figure out where I can play football because my school did not have any sports because of how small it was there were roughly 250 students for the whole school. So I found out that I am going to play for Hope High School.

I remember showing up during the summer as it was kind of a check in for paperwork and what we need before the season starts, and I remember one kid said to me that I look like easy work. Little did he know.

10th grade started and I showed up to practice every day after school got out, and I had to walk across town or take the bus depending on how much time I had. It was two miles away so it was part of my exercise before practice. During the fall it was almost like my zen. I woke up, went to school and rushed to practice to get out on that field. My first year playing high school football was like watching the movie Little Giants, no organization, no effort from the kids I mean it was a little crazy. We had talent, do not get me wrong and there was a lot of work cut out for us. That first year we won 2 games and sheesh that was rough. I made friends outside of the school that I went to and it was cool, people I talk to this day from time to time.

That same year in 10th grade around my birthday I was acting up, I just didn't want to listen to John or Julie at all. In school my grades were not up to par and I was getting into an argument with John at our place on the east side of Providence. He dumped water on me while I was on my bed, I wore nothing but a muscle shirt, sweatpants and socks. I got up from the bed and I ran outside and just kept going. We lived right behind Brown University's football stadium, I ended up on the other side of town closer to the North End of Providence. I had seen John drive by in his truck a couple times looking for me, I just kept ducking and moving. I had asked some people for some change near the area to make a phone call from a pay phone. One was to my friend Kenny at the time because we were planning to see Iron Man for my birthday. So I told him I am on the run from my brother right now and probably not going to be able to watch the movie.

After all that walking and running for a couple miles, I ended up calling my brother to let him know where I was and he picked me up. I was grounded, ended up going to the movies for my birthday and that was that.

Now I spend my summers really hanging out with friends, playing basketball, getting high, drinking alcohol.

11th grade back at it again with football and practice, this time I am a captain for the team and getting more vocal and talking with the coaches with more confidence and some of the schemes we can work out against teams and so forth. Yet another 2 win season.

Something happened during 11th grade and I am not sure what had happened and what snapped in my head but I was arguing and lying to my brother John and Julie. Before summer had started I was planning a road trip with a couple of my friends to head to South Carolina because of a dance competition he was in. Well I lied to my family that there was going to be an adult to drive down with us and that we were picking them up in Connecticut. Well it was just three of us at the time, and we were all going to take turns driving at some point. And I did not sleep the whole way down and it was my turn to drive. I fell asleep driving in North Carolina, I woke up driving in the median and woke up screaming "Oh Shit! Oh Shit! Oh Shit! Oh Shit! Oh Shit!" The car did not have any side mirrors, and needed the axels to be replaced, Luckily the repairs were paid for by Nolan's grandmother and fixed. After spending some time in North and South Carolina, all I could think of how shitty and fucked up that was to do that and drive back up to Rhode Island without telling my family. Well the rest of the summer I would spend time away from home and stay at my other friend Kenny's house with his family. One day I woke up one morning being woken up by Kenny's mother that John and his girlfriend were there and I was like what?

"We're going home now!" John says.

We are back home and he tells me to take a shower and that I need to get a job. Nolan had left a message over the house phone about paying back the money for the damage the car had after I had driven it. At that point I felt there was tension because of the lies I had given, and the danger I could have been in if people were hurt. As the summer went on I ended up leaving my brother's place and was staying with a couple of friends that had graduated from Textron already. I was living with Brandyn, Nate and his godfather who was a priest named Ken. So I ended up living on Vandewater Ave in Providence, which was not far from where my brother and I had lived originally on Coggeshall.

The summer before my senior year I didn't really speak to any of my family, occasionally I would speak with Ryan, I did not have James's contact information and at this point John and I were not really talking after I left.

Here comes my senior year in high school and

it's my final year competing in football not knowing what was happening afterwards. There was so much going on between going to school because everyone had heard what I did that summer. I was a leader to my friends on the football team who looked up to me because they respected who I was and didn't bullshit them. Whatever was happening outside of football did not present itself on the field during practice and games. I would sometimes bring some of the players back to my place and we would hang out and eat and I would drop them off at their home. My senior year at Hope High school we ended up in the playoffs, lost in the first round and went 7-1 and tied as co-champs of Division IV with Middletown High School, and Exeter West Greenwich High School. That year was one of my favorite years and I won't forget it. I would say in practice that if anyone started acting up I would tell the coach to make us run laps because we weren't taking it seriously. One of my teammates apologized to me after the playoff game because he was not taking practice seriously and knew how much it meant to us seniors.

For the playoff game my uncle Tim and my father showed up to the game as support and was one of the few times someone came to my game that year.

Well my senior year could not have gone crazier, I ended up in the Providence Journal, and on the local Channel 12 news. I had gotten letters to play football, yet I did not know what any of this meant. I was unsure of what I wanted to do after high school, I mean I guess go to college but to do what. I wanted to play college football at that point but again I need to attend college, where do I go and what do I do?

Later my senior year I was in biology class and I was called down to the front office, and there was an older man standing in the fourier (where people waited to be buzzed in once they confirmed the person was safe to come into the school). He was pointing at me to go see him, and so I went over there and had this curious look on my face as to who this man was.

Well turns out that he was a former Rhode Island State Trooper, who had a picture of my mother when she had gotten arrested for a bounced check. In addition, the Providence Journal copy of when I was in the newspaper, tells me that I have a sister.

I am sorry what? I got upset and after he left I just cried.

I really do not remember what I had said to him or even if I had said my name and maybe just in confusion as to how I have a sister and no one has told me after all this time.

Was this true?

When I had gotten home, I called Ryan, my father, and John. They all confirmed that I have a sister.

Ok no one was going to tell me? What in the actual fuck? Why wouldn't anyone tell me? Did I really piss everyone off that they weren't going to tell me?

Well nothing was made of it, none of them discussed it any further, no one knew anything and that was it.

One day I woke up to someone ringing the doorbell at the house on Vandewater Street, I opened the window from the 3rd floor to look out and there were 3 police officers and said "Hello, is Ken there?" I said no and they asked if I could come down and talk to them. I went downstairs and they asked if they could come up and talk. Well it was just Brandyn and myself there and we were separated and one of the officers came to ask me "had Ken had touched you in any way and if there was any weird activity that I was aware of?".

I said "hell no that man did not touch me. I do not know of anything going on."

Saw on the news a couple days later one of Ken's friends had gotten arrested for child molestation and child pornography, days later Ken committed suicide.

Mind was blown, what in the world was going on. I was living with this person and he could have had something to do with that. My friend Brandyn and I were so confused, what in the world do we do? Can we still live here?

At my high school graduation, I was happy to see that my family showed up to celebrate a big moment in my life at that point. I had thought that I had pissed off my brother and my father that I didn't deserve for them to be there. Just because I had lied, stole money, and I could have hurt people falling asleep at the wheel.

I had decided to go to the Talent Development program at the University of Rhode Island. Talent Development allowed students to get credits during the summer and I decided to leave because there were too many people that I knew and did not want to go to school with everyone I knew. Between the high school that I went to and my friends from Hope High school it just felt out of place for me. Or maybe I just was not ready for college yet. I never really took high school seriously enough between studying, actually learning the techniques of writing an actual paper, and math came easy to me so it was whatever. There was one teacher in school whose desk was just a mess and had a pile of papers, and he had asked me if I had completed an assignment. I had told him that I had put it on his desk, knowing damn well he was not going to look for it on his desk. I never completed the assignment.

One day a woman reached out to me on Facebook asking if we could meet, and we did at the Providence Place Mall food court. Her name was Eileen. Eileen had pictures of my sister, exchanged contact information and later that day I met my sister Kayley.Eileen had adopted my sister when she was at a very young age. Eileen, Kayley, and Tyler, my sister's brother and I all went to a restaurant called Gregg's in Warwick, RI.

Woah, my sister is also black! What? How? Well

this is interesting. I see a person of color who is living with a family that is white. Sound familiar? Either way, what?! I have a sister, this is awesome, she is younger than man and I hope this is a relationship that I can build with. There was not much for talking as we obviously had just met and did not really know what to say to each other. I had brought some photos of our mother, and brothers, for her to take a look at and keep some, I know Eileen and Tyler were observing our interactions as well supporting Kayley. This was one of those moments where I felt selfish and did not want to share this moment with anyone because this was special.

I was invited to live in Wakefield, RI, with Eileen, Kayley, and Tyler for a little bit, I had gone to school at Johnson and Wales, and CCRI by this time. I was still trying to figure out what I wanted to do and I still had no clue what that was. I was still struggling because I was really unsure of my passions and what I really enjoyed doing. I had felt the pressure from my-self that I had to show and be something to everyone, especially to my sister Kayley. No one told me to make sure I set an example, but I wanted to be something to someone at that point and time and I couldn't live up to it. I stopped going to school, lied about going to school, and just continued to work at Staples.

Then I had moved to Providence, RI, I had been working for Staples in Wakefield for some time now and transferred to the Providence store. I was living in an apartment with random people that I never met, because I needed a place to live. I would keep beer on my head board of my bed just to drink because I was bored at times. Only hung out with certain people still trying to figure out what I am doing with my life at this point. One of the other roommates had been arrested because he had sexually assaulted a little girl. This was all speculation because I just heard the police knocking on the third floor door and they had come barging in. I told myself that I needed to get the hell up out of there and I knew that I did not want to work at Staples forever and that I wanted to do something to one day impact someone's life. Whether that would be directly or indirectly. I still struggled to figure out what that was and how to do it, so hanging out with friends, drinking and smoking weed is what I was doing. I have had arguments with what seemed like with everyone in my family it seems and nothing has seemed to be getting better for myself. It was a dark time in my life where I just couldn't really pull it together, struggled to find passion and motivation. Went to clubs and got drunk with friends, drove when I should not have been driving, when everything I saw was blurry.

At one point in my life I was dating a woman around my age who had gotten pregnant, and she decided that she wanted to have an abortion. At that point in my life I would not say that I was numb but if she wanted to have the child I would have stepped up to be a father. Life decisions not only make an impact in your life, but others as well. I was 20 years old at the time and if we both decided to have that child I would have an older child by now and who knows what I would have been doing. Would I have finished school? Would I be struggling to provide for my child? So many questions that I have asked myself and wondering what my future would have looked like. Not only the impact of my life but the impact it may have left for her to have that abortion.

After going to University of Rhode Island, Johnson and Wales University both North Miami and Providence campuses, Community College of Rhode Island, Rhode Island College, and National University I have achieved my Bachelor's degree in Health Sciences, and My Master's in Public Health. Through all the crap that I have been through, through all the crap I put myself into, I was able to accomplish what I never thought was actually possible at moments in my life. It was one of the toughest journeys and I am still learning. I have an amazing and beautiful wife, my son who has just kept my motivation at a higher level than before.

After 29 years I found out that I have another sister! When I had received a message from Megan, I thought it was just another one of those spam or scam messages. In my head I am like either someone is pulling a prank on me or this is just nonsense like no one could have possibly gone this long without telling me I had another sister. Well this was real. Assuming no other surprises occur during my life of having another sibling out there, Megan was the first child my mother actually had. Maybe one day I will find out I have another family living on a different planet.

I have asked all those questions, what would it have been like if my mother was still alive? What if my mother and my biological father were together? Would I have brothers or sisters? What if? What if? What if? I can only handle what I can control. What if my father Michael had decided to not claim me as one of his own children, in which I am forever grateful for him doing that. At that moment he told me he wasn't my father, I felt that I needed to figure out who I was. I thought I had it figured out where I knew my mother, father, and my brothers. What if my brother decided not to have me live with him when my mother was diagnosed with cancer?

There were a lot of times in my life I would even ask what if I didn't exist anymore, would it be easier? The mental battle in my head that I didn't want to be stressed anymore. Feeling stressed most of my life because of the pressure I have put on myself to be the best that I can be. So that I never ended up like my mother, so that I can be the greatest parent, the greatest husband, sibling, son or whatever. Because everyday no matter what, it seems my mother was battling something and I felt that. I felt that I was carrying that stress because I never saw a consistency of happiness, or her being proud of her own life. There were peaceful moments when she would cook, especially birthday cakes. I remember her making baseball and football designed cakes from scratch. My favorite was her lemon meringue pie, and I never had another lemon meringue pie since she passed away. There are things that happen to you that can shape you who you are but it may not define you at all times.

I have had an instance where I was with my sister and a couple of my friends, I was driving, a person speeds right up next to us and just screams from his car "you fucking nigger!" I so badly wanted to chase the guy and beat his ass, but restrained myself because I thought of the consequences and with others being there as well.

At Staples, that is where I met Kristina in 2011, my now wife, we were just friends at that point nothing serious. But who knew that a connection would be made from working with someone that would change my life for the better. I wanted to become a better person not just for myself but to her as well because of the commitment that I have made. Having a son that makes life that much sweeter to enjoy and to help find his passions as well. There are moments every day that I cherish with my family because it's always something new and exciting to keep me motivated.

You may ask how I continued to push forward and not end up on the wrong side of life. I could have sold drugs, made money that way and not spend money to go to college to achieve something. I could have been stuck working at Staples for the rest of my life and deal with customers who want to complain about the price of ink cartridges. My father Michael, inspires me, for the mere fact he kept me as one of his own and never said to me that I wasn't his son. My brothers for always doing what they wanted and not a care in the world what others thought. My Sister Kayley from the day that we met, I have always wanted to be better to be her inspiration but she has been my inspiration. My sister Megan and her adventure. Kristina inspires me, because I want nothing for her but to be happy. Shea Jr., your smile, laugh, and infectious energy will never get old. I thrive off seeing people being happy, laugh, and enjoy what they are doing. Seeing friends and family do wonderful things, and doing it because they love it and puts a smile on their face is nothing greater.

Every single day I had a feeling of making a difference, unsure how I was going to do that. I struggled to find passions in my life that would push me over the hump to achieve something. I achieved my bachelors degree at the age of 27 years old. I was working, and going to school at the same time because I didn't know what I wanted after high school and I was not prepared to go to college right out of high school. It wasn't a great time for me. Once I found my groove in college, I went right into my Master's program in Public Health and it felt it was the right time, and that I wanted nothing more at that point in my life. I was learning what I wanted to learn, to become something in this world that could make a difference. I may not be making differences directly, but indirectly. I know if I wanted to be a police officer, truck driver, or a doctor,I know I could do it, but is that what I really want to do. What is your passion? You may not know what that is at this given point, are what you are doing now going to get you where you want to be?

I wanted to create this book to really help those who may be struggling to find it within to moti-vate themselves to accomplish things that they never thought they could. A lot of what I have done was by having the self pressure to have to do it on my own. A lot of it was being ignorant, naive, and hard headed. There were also people in my life trying to point me in the right direction and I never saw it that way. I saw it as if people were telling me what to do and it wasn't. I always asked myself when I was younger what I wanted to be when I grew up. After my mother had passed it felt to me internally that I needed to learn how to survive. I am talking about surviving mentally and how I wanted to live my life. I had felt that I just grew up watching my mother struggle. I knew that I did not want to struggle my entire life and wanted to live a life of happiness and whatever it meant by that. Not all the money in the world was not going to solve that problem, I understood hard work was going to take me places, but I questioned how that was going to happen. I also wanted to make a difference but unsure what that was going to look like. There are many ways to make a difference, whether that would be this book, becoming a doctor, nurse, teacher, motivational speaker, an influencer etc. There are decisions every day that you will make that could make an everlasting factor in your future. No, your favorite pizza that you eat today will not decide whether or not you will own a pizza shop. But hanging out with certain people during and after school, if you decide to play sports, engage in after school activities, or even teachers in school. I have had teachers tell me all the time that I was smart, and sometimes it was like ok cool but what does that even mean? Did that mean I was the smartest student they knew? I am completely fine with who I am, and the challenges life brings daily, that is what makes me who I am. The reason I'm Perfect the way that I am.

No one wakes up wanting to fail, it's a matter of how you want to succeed and define your success. My journey is still going.

What will yours be?

CPSIA information can be obtained
at www.ICGtesting.com
Printed in the USA
LVHW080728291222
735836LV00008BA/753